Nodus Tollens

Ceanna Tess Moormans

Presentation by *BookLeaf Publishing*

Web: www.bookleafpub.com

E-mail: info@bookleafpub.com

ISBN: 9789363304000

First edition 2024

ACKNOWLEDGEMENT

Because of my family, who regularly watch my stars implode and still keep sitting in the dust together with me, challenging me to look to the Sun.

For all those who struggle to put it into words, who struggle even to breathe.

And because of the greatest Word that ever was. (John 1:1-5)

PREFACE

"I hate writing!"

Or so I adamantly thought. As a little girl, I hated any assignment that had me take out a pen and paper. It was boring, dull, and laborious. I couldn't understand why anyone would choose to write. The moment I understood that writing is as much a creative art form as dance or acting was the moment I changed my mind. I remember a dance class that compared art to the "steril" written word, and it completely changed my perspective. To understand a person fully, one must consider their entire character. As a right-brained individual who loves dance, art, and acting, I initially struggled with the idea of comparing dance to writing. My teachers encouraged me to see movement as storytelling, and this perspective shift led me to realize the artistry and power of words. From journaling as a child to creating comic strips and personal narratives, I soon discovered that writing could be enjoyable and liberating. Recognizing writing as a powerful form of expression transformed my view of it from a tedious task to an essential part of my life. Now, I embrace my evolving identity as a writer—one who learns, connects, and expresses creatively. I'm proud to say I love "dancing" across pages, celebrating the writer I have become and continue to aspire to be.

In the process of assembling this little collection, in good old Tess-fashioned way, I forgot to hit save and lost all my work right before the last page.

And I mean everything.

There was no small part of me that wanted to rip all my hair out, close my computer, and quit.

After having my mini meltdown (and no, it wasn't pretty), I took a second to appreciate the frustratingly unpredictable, temporal, and temporary nature of life. I had to laugh about what a perfect analogy it was for everything I was trying to communicate through my poems. "Nodus Tollens" The realization that the plot of your life doesn't make sense to you anymore. There is a sense of loss of control that is liberating. I humbly resigned myself to reality and calmly began writing again (Ha, who are we kidding? I furiously poured out everything I could remember and some of what I could not as fast as I could. It was a deliciously bittersweet aftertaste of my anger).

Jokes aside. Somehow, that description prefaces this book better than I could have prior. It's a collection of wrestlings. It's imperfect. Writing from pure memory and repetition, I'm not sure all the words are as flawlessly seamless as before. I'm not even sure they are all there. But they are wild, changing, and real. I know the guts of them are spilled on the pages.

Maybe the first time, it was just meant for me—a sort of living diary and an exercise in putting one's full heart into something even though it didn't last. This time I'm curious what you'll read. What's the aftertaste that lingers?

Ad Astra per Aspera

~ s t a r d u s t ~

Dirt and light entwine in an intimate dance

Not a big bang,

but oh, what an explosion of existence!

One must have known the opportunity
being birthed,

the heartbreak,
beauty,
agony,

mirth.

The inner turmoil ignited,

the gift yet gifted.

and our independence transmitted.

The choice was ours,

look up and remember the Sun

breathed deep in the wells of our vagus,

Or allow gravity to encumber;

to pull down our stars

and permit the ground to plague us.

This must be why there is no oxygen in the
skies,

to choose one means the other's demise.

Mere dirt cannot stroll down the Milky Way,

but neither can light fall to the ground
without erupting in glorious flames.

This is the beautiful irony of being a
Lightling;

to live on the earth, so many ails

yet long for a higher terrain.

Worse still,

to remember the light

but cling to the night, dirt-caked nails

mud infiltrating our veins.

It is pondered whether there is life beyond
us.

But there exists hardly a more paradoxical
thought

when one realizes,

it is the only life that ever was.

Did you know Aurora Borealis means

"Breath of Dawn"?

Bereshit Elohim, enephusesen.

Mental Barriers

5

It is exhausting to be so acutely self-aware

and yet such a prisoner, chained to my mind.

I am both the victim and the witness

to my own crimes.

My thoughts have such a captive audience

the world's best stages could never dream.

It's as if I, the inmate

stand outside the cell

begging for entry, I'm already free.

And Me

The wind howls through the trees,

The ground quakes with color,

The trees shudder in the shadows,

And me.

My mind falls to its knees,

My heart aches in wonder,

My eyes in fearsome glow,

Because you decreed

in all your glory, majesty, and immortality

the audacity

of me.

Control Freak

I know exactly what I want

and how it should go,

all the people and places

and what they should know.

I know what I'd do and what I definitely would not,

I have life all figured out

in a neat, tidy box.

High on my pride, I tout touching lives.

The elusive swell takes stride, and then I realize

what if the only place that I did

was my mind.

In my mind, I'm a hero.

(But it's only my mind).

What if all the things I've hated

can only be seen by someone equally as
self-deceived,

deceptive, and jaded?

*What if, at the end of that alluring race to
perfection,*

I look back and find

my life was nothing more

than a stale art collection?

Actions speak louder than words, so they say,

*but somehow words are the only feeble move I
continue to make.*

And so pen clenched in fist,

I keep watching the strokes curl into shapes.

I know exactly what I want,

or so I thought.

Looking back

everything I wanted

is everything

I'm not.

What a tragedy to awake and realize,

I was given everything

and still found my demise.

There is no glory in suffering

caused by one's own foolish design.

Stability.

Consistency.

Routine.

The only comfort that exists is knowing things will change,

the only terror is the same.

Drowning

Once I walked on sandy shores

next to me, the seafoam roared.

It beckoned me to heed its song

to race the birds and play along.

I thought I understood its cry

a melancholy lullaby.

It cooed of wonders never seen

It tempted, urged,

dared one to dream.

But as my eyes welled in the salty breeze,

another thought came to me.

The sheets of water white as snow

beg the sand for a place to go.

The rainbow of colors never rests

for all these years, it never slept.

Chasing gold already possessed inside

its jealous passion is seen in the tide.

I realized as I anthropomorphized the
waters blue,

my vivid thoughts turned to You.

The Creator of the foamy seas, chases, bleeds, and

died for me.

Fierce as a raging storm yet gentle,

Your love ebbs and flows immortal.

Never yielding,

never still,

we are saturated,

drowned,

yet never forced against our will.

Your world had everything you ever needed,

but somehow it wasn't enough without

me in it.

The Monster Under My Bed
(Or was it all in my head?)

When asked what I fear,

I smile and talk about tight spaces or crowded halls,

I am claustrophobic after all.

Any number of ordinary things,

routinely cavalier,

I lightheartedly begin to list them each:

When I was a girl, I hated the dark,

scary movies,

clowns, and sharks.

Pain and needles

Tornados, bees,

and other creepy crawly things.

Getting in trouble,

the monster under my bed,

being sick or

missing time with my friends.

When it was time to go to sleep,

I hated what would be in my "dreams."

I'd always ask to crack the door,

"Keep alert for any creaking on the floor."

"There is no monster hiding there."

Mommy would soothe and pat my hair.

But what I really fear goes mostly unsaid.

I'm afraid of me,

I'm the walking dead.

Longing for the vulnerable and deep,

*I somehow always keep to the superficial and
cheap.*

Even in my fears, I'm desperate to be admirable,

beautiful.

You see,

*I'd rather battle the most terrifying villain of any
horror*

than face the reflection in the mirror,

in the corner.

I hate to fail and fall

and I'd do anything to keep you from seeing me

how I see me.

There is a monster after all.

It lives here in the house rent-free,

but it's not in the closet or under my bed.

It's me.

Yes, I am claustrophobic.

gasping for breath,

I'm suffocating.

A Blistered Breath

A sweet song

screamed aloud,

a melody painfully present.

What could I say that could match the tone;

a holy body, broken from heaven.

I strive and
I cry and
I wonder,
"why?"
but in a moment
I suddenly realize...

Not a single word could suffice,

not a symphony of confessions,

a whole lifetime of writing hymns of
repentance.

Only one thing, without the need of a sound
at all;

a life of being,

actions that unquestionably answer the call.

A sweet song screams aloud,

a harmony, distinct, yet unified.

Who could say enough to match the tune?

We are the body,

once bruised,

buried,

now alive.

Requiem

You know how they say your whole world flashes
in front of you right before you die?

Well, I saw this once, and I'm still alive...

Or am I?

Recipe for Love

There isn't one.

Wait a Minute

27

Hold on for a minute

don't do anything else.

You can look at a clock,

or begin counting,

60 seconds, starts now.

....
Ok,

I'd wager you're expectant

or else

somewhat annoyed,

or curious,

thereabouts.

*You see, waiting does wonders the rush never
could.*

In waiting, we're forced to reexamine

what we were sure we already understood.

In waiting there's beauty

most do not see,

as irresistible as the respite breath of fresh air

amid an arduous journey.

But we're "too busy."

Think of all the things that simply beg us to
wait;

The measure of rest on a cream-colored page,

that makes way for the dramatic crescendo to
fill the stage.

The pause before a kiss,

When you look in their eyes

its subtle intimacy,

you would be remiss to despise,

and to gloss over would surely be a terrible
sacrifice.

There's a calm in the storm

before destruction wages war.

*And the periods on paper that command even
more.*

Such power lies in the small little slash and dot.

one that controls when you breathe

and when you cannot.

Words are just alphabet soup on a page,

until forced to find order,

and ordered to rearrange.

There's the second of hesitation,

deafening silence before a sea of applause.

To clap too soon would be a

faux pas.

There is love in the waiting

the waiting of ordinary things.

I often see this in my ivory piano keys.

They quietly wait to be touched.

They are there when I caress them

and still when I do not.

Or think how a mug patiently

waits for coffee to fill it

warmed deep inside,

the steamy hug transmitted.

On the mantle in my parent's room,

there is a poem I often read:

"Walk a little slower, Daddy."

The first few lines speak.

And I have to agree.

There is love in waiting,

and I love those who wait for me.

There is a lover, He waited too

He wants to be seen,

He's waiting for you.

And he waits until he bleeds,

until he died on a tree.

In fact, he is still waiting in the spaces

in between.

Think back to the beginning

A minute felt long

I'd wager you didn't make it,

you skipped right through,

Even just sixty seconds is too much

for you, (and me too).

But next time you're tempted to hurry on by,

remember most of life is waiting.

All of us are just waiting,

then we die. (Or find new life)

T'i, me and Bye

Time passes by
Ti e passe by
   me pass   by
   i   pas   by
              by
              bye

La Ventana

La Ventana

Recuerdo el dia cuando la ví;

simple,

pero hermosa

atrás de donde dormí.

Y justo afuera

una linda mirada;

un arbol rosa

alta y orgullosa.

Y al otro lado

una pared,

resistente, gris y seca

así como quién tiene mucha sed.

Fue un tipo de cuadro hermoso

que nunca imaginé

tan contrastado

la imagen mental nunca la borraré.

Después de un tiempo

Me di cuenta de algo más.

La próxima vez que vi detrás

Nada de la vista cambió

pero mi perspectiva

la ventana

casi quebró.

La misma pared

el mismo árbol,

pero la vista anterior

desapareció.

y en lugar del retrato lindo

una chica

pequeña ,

encarcelada

sin ver el sol.

Quisiera estar enojada

con la ventana

por la belleza que me robó.

Pero la única que cambió

fui yo.

Home

Home

/hōm/

Feeling

1. Such a foreign and familiar place all at once.

An eerie contradiction of a word.

Tears of Rain

Pitter pitter-pat

I hear the soothing rhythm on my window glass.

My mind's eye is caught wandering through the tunnels of time,

now the physical one turns its gaze to the drops racing by

as I observe the watery struggle engulfed in indigo

the streaks scuttle, then stop, and then they let go.

They blaze endless trails, imperfect and jagged

much like my own, so full of baggage.

My thoughts chase the droplets in an endless
maze

drowning in memories—both of beauty... and
pain.

I first cheer for one, then squeal for the other,

then they blur and together plummet downward.

They invite me to join them,

to accept, release, and free fall.

I escape my brain's conundrums

by embracing them all.

To the great, wide open.

I escape outdoors.

It's dirty but beautiful

this fresh air petrichor.

And as my heart touches the damp earthy tones,

I am invited to dance through the deluge that comes.

Slipping and sliding

then completely at rest

I realize in the distance, the thunder's in check.

P i t t e r,   p i t t e r,   pat.

I hear the soothing rhythm on my window glass

slower now, forcing me to ask;

Did the drops belong to the pane or to me?

In watching them fall,

I set myself free.

And with a blurry gaze, my vision is clear,

the drops streaming down are my very own tears.

My soul's windows shine bright

as clarity is found through the pain.

Outside in the sun's rays,

it's just beginning to rain.

The Great What If

What if it were all different?

What if you weren't you

What if all the things you despised were

suddenly untrue.

Would it finally be enough?

Would we ever be satisfied?

Or would we find a myriad of other reasons
to cry?

Such a powerful grasp;

What should be

what it could be

and all the maybes in between.

You ever wonder

if what should have been is exactly what is?

Are we all just our own worst enemies?

Deep

I don't know how to do anything softly.

Everything

is deep and deeply overwhelming.

There is a part of me that would die for all the lives

I'll never live.

Eventide

49

What a tragedy it takes a life to learn how to live.

Only, maybe that's the point.

This is practice.

For something higher,

Something better.

Rejoice.

11:59

11:59 pm.

In one moment, or

sixty seconds, or

sixty-thousand milliseconds

today will be gone,

and today will be yesterday,

and tomorrow will be today.

It's kind of terrifying when you think about it.

Terrifying in the way that everything you
did today

—all the lists you've made,

places you've been,

things you've touched,

songs you've heard,

conversations you've had

—will soon become a memory,

or worse, it would become forgotten.

Lost amidst all your yesterdays.

gone.

12:00 am.

Today.

9 789363 304000